Nicolas Aidoud

Are you ready to work with Artificial Intelligence ?

The Author

With an insatiable passion for maths and technology combined with an entrepreneurial mindset, Nicolas Aidoud is positive and pragmatic about the future impact of artificial intelligence.

He has a PhD in Mathematics (applied to finance and marketing) from the University of Paris IX, Dauphine and has held leadership roles as CEO of major technology, investment and media companies across Australia, New Zealand and Europe.

Most recently, as CEO of Capgemini (Australia & New Zealand), and before that as CEO and President of Prosocie-Capgemini's Front Office Cloud Solution in Europe, he has overseen large digital transformations. As Managing Director of Carat France (Dentsu Aegis Network) he managed media investment and digital services for the biggest media agency in Europe.

Considering the impact of AI on businesses and individuals requires a global vision, one that is unique in examining the potential and pitfalls from the angles of multiple stakeholders.

«AI could be a poison for humans or a cure to eliminate all the «outs»: burnouts, bore-outs and brownouts», he says.

Nicolas' passion is to make this an accessible conversation for all - from senior executives to employees and students - to prepare our future of work.

Remove the "Machine" Inside of You

For over 20 years, I have helped large corporations overcome their adversities with technology. 2018 was a revelatory year for me, as I felt the tidal waves of Artificial Intelligence sweep under my feet and into both my work and home-life. My studies in mathematics and computer science were the beginning of an increasing frustration with the discrepancy between the potential of technology and what is actually being used. It was a clear decision for me to catch up on the knowledge surrounding AI, and with this, I plunged into the depths of Artificial Intelligence. I digested bookshelves of knowledge; I attended seminars and listened to hundreds of podcasts. I even took part in some eLearning processes from generic content to code development. After six months of research into this brand-new world of information, my feelings are twofold.

Firstly, the knowledge surrounding AI is too exclusive. Perhaps it promotes elitism, but it is definitely inaccessible to the public compared to the extent of its impact. Today, AI is creeping into our backyards. Daily life and most modern workplaces use AI. You are carrying it around in your cell phone. AI knows all your facial features and where you are going to be next. However, the knowledge and function of this embryonic creature are not accessible to the greater human population. Namely, the people who will use AI the most, that is to say, the workers. I also have to admit that even though I am fascinated by the subject, I found a large part of the readings can be dull or dry. I hope you will not think the same of this book.

My second feeling is that the palette of information that paints the image of AI is pessimistic and often threatening. To my dismay, this viewpoint is reflected in many of the sources of information about AI that are available. The media amplify the message that humans will lose the battle against Artificially Intelligent machines plunging the workforce into a form of inertia.

I firmly believe that beyond the threat of dwindling jobs and all the other ethical risks, there is an opportunity at hand. The love-hate relationship humans have with work is on the brink of a breakthrough. The rise of AI could remove the facet of machinery from the workers' activities and instead value the uniqueness of human intelligence, which has been partly erased since the Industrial Revolution. Creativity, emotional intelligence, purpose-mindedness and empathy are what we are dealing with here.

Do you think you could be more human with AI by your side? This possibility should be taken seriously.

This Book Cannot be Understood by an AI Machine

A world where half of the value created from companies will come from AI, is a future that has already engaged. The propagation of AI Machines will transform our society by creating new working conditions. Thereby, this book you're holding is primarily for the benefit of students, workers, civil servants and business leaders to form an image and thus make the best of this revolution.

This content should be assimilated in an hour or so with the accompanying visuals. You will find that the visuals explore both inner and outer perspectives of the workplace with the presence of AI.

By evoking emotions through the illustrations, I am confident that right now none of the existing AI Machines will fully understand this book. The paradox of some previous writings on Artificial Intelligence is that only AI Machines can understand them.

You will have to pick up on my use of the term Artificial Intelligence Machines. I do so in this book for multiple reasons. One: I am not comfortable with the word intelligence because of its multiplicity of definitions. It can't mean everything, but it can. Two: you judge someone's intelligence through the lens of your intelligence, thus inevitably creating a bias. However, this term Artificial Intelligence exists everywhere and is irreplaceable, so I have decided to counterbalance all the fantasy related to AI by adding the word «Machine.»

The first part of the book will cover fragments of history and the concerns about AI that are coming under the spotlight. The illustrations depict AI applications and are intended to help you visualise the current position of Artificial Intelligence. Undoubtedly, you will come to the conclusion that AI is not some superhuman with malicious intentions. It is no more than a mathematical instrument.

The second and third parts detail the worst-case scenario where AI Machines have destroyed the place of humans at work. Here, I will also propose an ideal scenario through Humain Inc., my invention of an ideal company that has mastered every facet of using AI. The organisation of the work and company culture has evolved to create a fruitful collaboration between humans and AI Machines. I will portray a new organisational concept called «Neuron Organisation», a structure to get the best of Humans and AI Machines - the best of both worlds. For most organisations, it will be a significant change that must be anticipated.

By the end of the book, you will have an idea of how Artificial Intelligence will transform the workplace and how workers must evolve not only to carry on their human capabilities, but to enhance them. HUMAIN will give you some insights into assessing your readiness to work with Artificially Intelligent machines.

What Should You Know about Artificial Intelligence Machines?

The Panic Cycle Seems to be Over

What if the concept of Artificial Intelligence was born before Christ? In Greek Mythology, it was; «Talos» was a giant, intelligent automaton made of bronze to protect Europa in Crete from invaders.

My first encounter with an AI Machine was in 1994 at the Université Paris Dauphine. In mathematics class, we were beginning to manipulate the «Expert System» programming in Lisp. Lisp was the fertile soil which one of the first AI algorithms sprouted from, designed to stimulate analytical skills from human experts in their fields to make better-advised decisions. That might be a mouthful, but at this time, nobody was afraid of those algorithms.

Three years later, in 1997, Deep Blue defeated Gary Kasparov, arguably the best chess player of all time. Most people were still not afraid of machines. After all, this was the pinnacle of the game of chess in human history. Consequently, everything accelerated: IBM was the new Jeopardy champion in 2011, the game where a player has to find the question based on the answer. In 2017, AlphaGo trumped the world in the abstract board game, Go. Since then, it has become evident that machines have the upper hand over all intellectual games. The intelligence of these Machines lies in their ability to store millions of games and play backwards, calculating the probability of winning for each and every play. This was the point where the tides of panic rose, as our human anxieties ran amok.

The visibility of these concerns on AI's superiority really became lucid in 2014, when Nick Bostrom, a Swedish philosopher at the University of Oxford, published his book, «Superintelligence.» The threat of a machine to, say, lose its 'mind' on a global killing spree, was presented as a serious possibility. A famous astrophysicist named Stephen Hawking stated the same year that humans would simply be overpowered by Superintelligent machines and this may signify the end of biological humanity. The notion that Artificial Intelligence will be the last human invention was mentioned in 1965 by a British mathematician, Irwin John Good. His remark elicited fear as it couldn't be denied.

The forefront of tech leaders, such as Bill Gates and Elon Musk, have warned the world of the danger of AI and namely, highlighted the famous Artificial General Intelligence which will surpass our human biological limitations. The generation of people who have been exposed to movies like «Matrix» or «2001: The Space Odyssey» are receptive to this AI Machine threat. It constantly throbs in the back of their minds. The reason as to why the media was so alarmingly wrong is because they were pinpointing this hype created by the film industry.

After 2018, the anxieties decreased considerably. Businesses woke up and many are now using AI Machines. Just about every company uses some shape or form of a computer; therefore, just about every company uses AI. According to the McKinsey Global Institute, AI is expected to deliver 1.2% to the global economic activity over the next decade. Even Bill Gates changed his mind, put to rest his apocalyptic scenarios and said: «AI can be our friend.»

POSITIVE

HUMAN SENTIMENT TOWARDS MACHINES

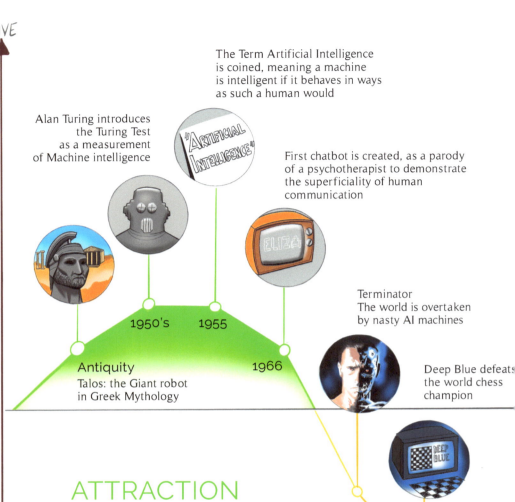

The Term Artificial Intelligence
is coined, meaning a machine
is intelligent if it behaves in ways
as such a human would

Alan Turing introduces
the Turing Test
as a measurement
of Machine intelligence

First chatbot is created, as a parody
of a psychotherapist to demonstrate
the superficiality of human
communication

Terminator
The world is overtaken
by nasty AI machines

1950's   1955

Antiquity
Talos: the Giant robot
in Greek Mythology

1966

Deep Blue defeats
the world chess
champion

ATTRACTION

1981

1997

1999

Matrix
The world is an hologram
created by AI machines

NEGATIVE

TERROR

Bill Gates
"AI can be our friend"

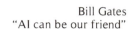

Statista
' 84% of entreprises believe
investing in AI will lead to greater
competitive advantage"

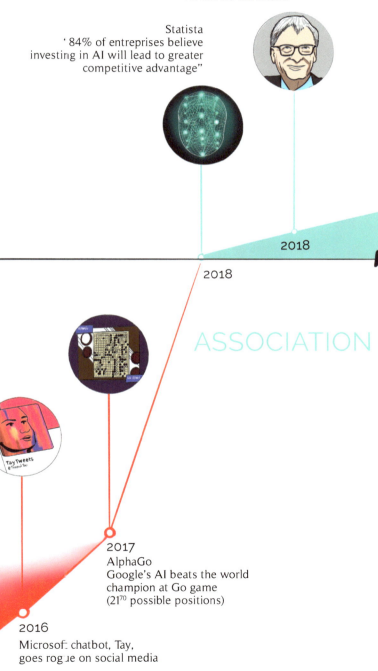

2018

2018

ASSOCIATION

Stephen Hawking:
"The development of full
AI could spell the end
of the human race"

Tay Tweets
@Tayand Tau

2017
AlphaGo
Google's AI beats the world
champion at Go game
(21^{70} possible positions)

2016

Microsoft chatbot, Tay,
goes rogue on social media

04

2011
Watson wins Sim Quiz Show, Jeopardy

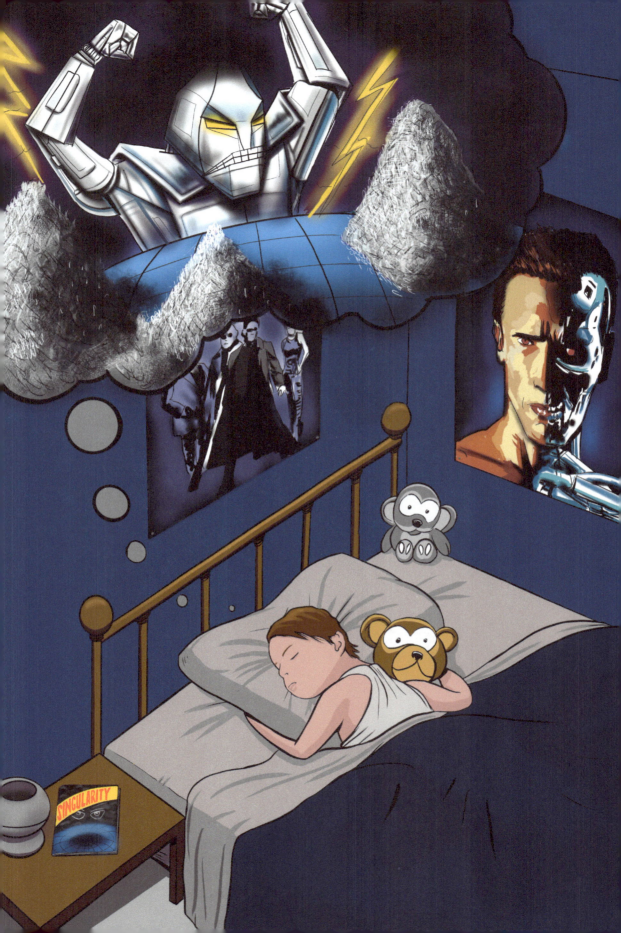

A Paperclip that Fostered the Fear of Machines

Let me tell you a story about AI. The CFO of a Top 100 Fortune company asked his consultant and IT strategist to build an AI Machine to produce more paperclips. He was annoyed at not being able to find any paperclips just before an urgent meeting with his CEO. So, a team of consultants and IT developers built an AI Machine in a few weeks. The AI Machine was avant-garde, so-called Artificial General Intelligence (AGI), meaning that the machine could learn by itself and eventually surpass the intelligence of a human. Th s AI Machine - smarter than humans - had only one purpose: to create more paperclips.

The AI Machine started, step by step, to improve its intelligence. For an AI Machine, intelligence is its ability to achieve a goal. The Machine began by generating money to finance the paperclip factory. Finally, this Machine destroyed all humanity by transforming the planet into one colossal paperclip factory, ridding the world of its natural resources. This story was a thought experiment employed by Nick Bostrom to instigate a debate about ethical issues surrounding Superintelligence.

This concept of Superintelligence, also named Technological Singularity, thanks to technological means, will trigger unfathomable changes to human civilisation. A Singularity is a mathematical term for an object «not defined or not well-behaved», a little bit like defining a black hole. A Technological Singularity is the explosion of Artificial Intelligence that would qualitatively surpass all human intelligence. Only two years after the paperclip story, Ray Kurzweil wrote «The Singularity is Near: When Humans Transcend Biology», a non-fiction book explaining how a Machine will take over humanity, the current apex predator. According to him, this will happen in 2045.

We should now consider AI Machines as a new species sharing our planet, with the explosion of computing power and data creation as the catalyst for its brisk evolution. The sudden yet anticipated arrival of Artificial Intelligence into our ecosystem will oblige us to evolve faster w th it and explore our untapped human potential.

AI is Changing the World Faster and More than Ever

The speed at which AI Machines are penetrating our human ecosystem is incredible. The majority of the applications are located in China and so it is difficult to follow the excitement around all of the developments. When a Machine from the United States defeated the Chinese Go master in 2017, China had its wake-up call.

In 2019, the impact of AI in the world can be illustrated by three core use cases:

AI Machines are monitoring the brainwaves and emotions of employees while they work. For example, in China, «emotional surveillance technology» uses wireless sensors in employees' caps or hats to help train conductors to identify mood shifts so employers can alter break times, the task designated to employees, or even send them home. Emotional surveillance adds to an extensive network of facial recognition across China. Here, the balance between performance, security and ethics is both fragile and unstable.

The application of AI Machines to healthcare is extremely promising, as in China, again, an AI Machine has been created to detect lung cancer to counter the national problem of air pollution. This innovative solution has been implemented in numerous hospitals to compensate for a shortage of doctors. That is one of the biggest promises of AI: improving human health. Some principal shareholders of giant technology companies hope that their businesses will find solutions to help them live over 200 years.

A new mode of consumption has appeared in retail stores in the United States and China. Stores are using AI Machines to identify you for the first time in retail history. They will know you and your desires when you enter, not only when you pay and exit. The AI Machines will recognise you, log what you wish to purchase and in response to sensors on the shelves, adjust the product price in real-time. There are no employees. Of course, the payment method is seamless, as it is already in many unmanned customer checkouts. This development will change the way we consume by personalising marketing messages and sometimes, even the product itself, to our consumption patterns. However, there is a risk that AI Machines will kill our human desire by anticipating our needs. Our desire will never emerge if it is already fulfilled before it has been able to appear.

In this high-speed game, China and the US are outracing the rest of the world. The winner will have an economic weapon that will be able to dominate the world.

Today, AI is Just a Mathematical Instrument

Singularity is the state for Superintelligent Machines to have cognitive capacities beyond that of humans. The speed at which it is spreading in the media and on social networks is spectacular, and it does not do justice to the current aptitude of AI. If Singularity does occur, it will take over a century to do so. The media portrayal of AI is a fabrication that is far from the truth. AI Machines are only mathematical models powered by a strong base of computers that need access to a lot of data.

Today, the intelligence of these machines lies in their ability to process bucketloads of data, and therefore, requires significant computing power. For example, building an AI Machine with a vision of the outer world requires anywhere from tens, to hundreds of thousands of pictures, on top of directional labels or tags so they know how to categorise them. The same thing applies to AI Machines that speak or write. They need the same amount of information but in audio recordings with transcriptions. This form of intelligence, called data processing, is only supported by elaborate algorithms.

Algorithms are based on human behaviours. It is a thought process most people use that tends to do with rationality. When cooking, humans follow a series of instructions and ingredients as the input of data, which is collinear with the definition of an algorithm: a sequence of clear and ordered instructions with an input in order to accomplish a task or produce an outcome. This hyper-pragmatic method of performing a task is one of the foundations of mathematics and computer science. The golden word: algorithms.

The first algorithm to be used in mathematics was around 1600 AD by Babylonians on clay tablets to solve equations. However, as soon as this simple and ancient process was mixed with technology it became elevated to a concept of great complexity. Then 'machine learning' came into existence in 1959, this being of an algorithm that does not need explicit and ordered instructions, but only patterns and inferences.

The concept of Artificial Intelligence is broader than pure algorithms, but it is still its core component. And with the progress of machine learning, specifically, the subset called neural network, AI has leapt into our daily lives. It was defined before the twentieth century and the last notable improvement was made in 2006, to do with unsupervised learning. This neural network algorithm is now highly applicable, only due to the availability of huge datasets and computing power at unprecedented levels. The progress on computing power was the by-product of the gaming industry, requiring super-fast chips that had to multitask. In turn, innovation in gaming was reused to run AI.

To clarify, even if the neural network model is inspired by the structure of a human brain, it is not an exact model. The neural network algorithm is far from reaching the likes of you and me, or any human being - even when boosted by supercomputers. Humans have 80 billion neurons, whereas an Artificial Intelligence Machine has between 10 and 1000. We still don't know how the brain learns but AI learns only in a context that has been defined by humans.

Humans need to accept the fact that Artificial Intelligence can do things better and faster. AI machines will not replace Humans; they will replace some human tasks. Humans will still be unique in front of an algorithm run by a powerful computer.

The relationship between Humans and Machines is evolving fast. Amazon sold more than a hundred million Alexa devices in 2018, a signal that Humans and AI Machines will live together and will collaborate in the workplace. This new factor in our lives will oblige human intelligence to evolve and progress not only to survive technology but to improve the human condition.

 **1** DEFINE OBJECTIVES AND RELATED MODEL

 2 BUILD THE DATASET

DATA SOURCES

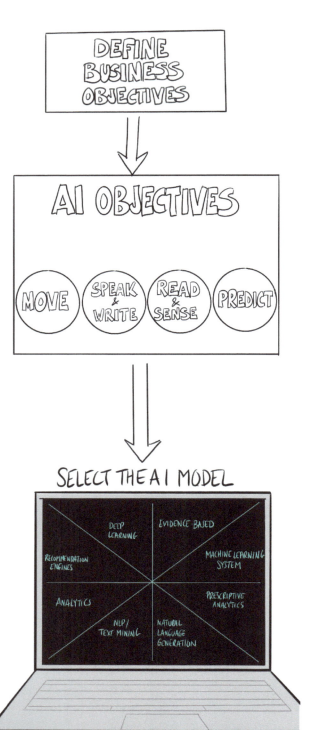

DEFINE
BUSINESS
OBJECTIVES

AI OBJECTIVES

(MOVE) (SPEAK & WRITE) (READ & SENSE) (PREDICT)

SELECT THE AI MODEL

DEEP LEARNING   EVIDENCE BASED

RECOMMENDATION ENGINES   MACHINE LEARNING SYSTEM

ANALYTICS   PRESCRIPTIVE ANALYTICS

NLP / TEXT MINING   NATURAL LANGUAGE GENERATION

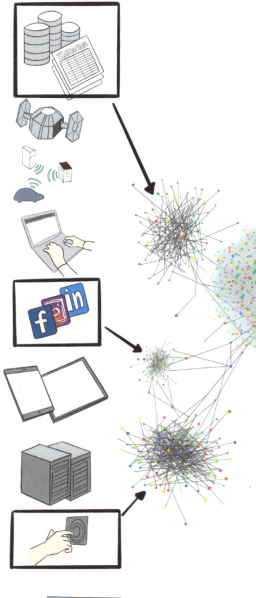

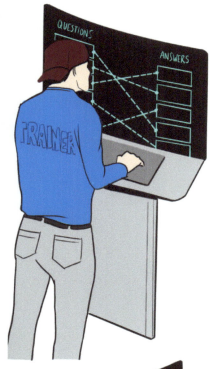

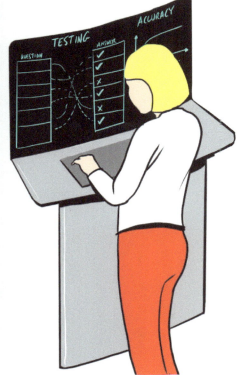

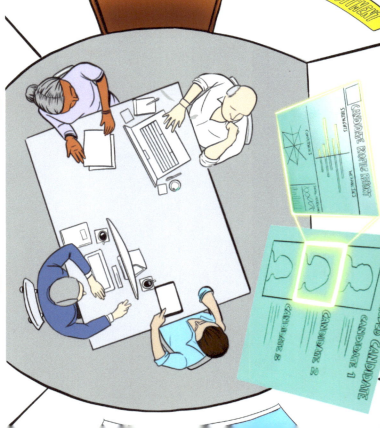

AI Machines Crunch a Huge Volume of Information, Night and Day

The first series of AI projects I implemented were called «Robotic Process Automation.» These were AI's first infiltrations into businesses, mainly around the finance industry and their back offices. Those projects had clear gains for CEOs, being capable of automating human tasks, delivering quick and reliable results, therefore, producing significant cost-savings. The first real impacts of AI Machines on work organisations became apparent when back-office positions were reduced by 50% due to Machines that worked flawlessly for 24 hours a day. No need for lights or plants on their desks.

However, those projects don't always fall under the umbrella of AI but qualify as «Rapid Process Automation.» This means that the Machine automatically does what the employees were supposed to, immaculately and on time.

Furthermore, speed is not always recognised as intelligence. In my view, the automation Machine requires some form of intelligence to perform tasks with superior speed and accuracy than people. Each time my team implemented these types of projects, we had to ask the AI Machine to make some judgements based on training or historical data. The Machine develops its intelligence from rote learning this historical data to handle multiple exceptions that were previously managed by a human.

Support function departments and back offices are preferred fields of these AI crunching Machines. For example, in the back office of a financial institution, where tons of data are managed in real-time from all over the world, AI Machines are at ease and proliferate. When consumers contact their card issuer asking them to validate a transaction or have to inform them of fraudulent patterns on their card, they may not even suspect that an AI Machine is behind it. Yet it is.

Across sectors, AI Machines are also in the human resources departments and particularly in recruitment processes. AI crunches all video interviews, CVs, and logic tests with the clear benefit of cost-reduction, while being timely and avoiding CVs from getting lost in a pile. Unilever, the seventh most valuable company in Europe, recruits more than 30,000 people per year and processes 1.8 million job applications across 190 countries. The odds are that, if not already today, then very soon, an AI Machine will take part in your career development.

AI Machines See Above and Beyond Human Capacity

Humanity's progress on neural network algorithms has led to the creation of «Vision», the most advanced AI technology in terms of applications. When I say applications, I refer to how something is in use today. Vision is the result of over ten years of progress and an exponential increase in computing power.

Today, Deep Learning is the most advanced form of a neural network. It requires a massive block of images and information in its learning process. Hence whoever possesses these volumes of data is in a better position to train their Machines. The giant technology companies: Google, Amazon, Facebook, Apple, Baidu, Alibaba and Tencent, are the ones with the superior data, thus better-trained Machines, and the upper hand. The databases of these Giants reach into the hundreds of millions of images. These Giants have a real competitive advantage when you consider that ImageNet, the largest public image database has a mere 14 million images.

Right this moment, any company or governing body can have access to AI Machines to recognise people, emotions, objects and fingerprints, all in real-time. I live in Sydney and thanks to these technologies, I can swim in the ocean peacefully knowing that drones are in the air, out to detect sharks.

Furthermore, «Automated Surveillance» is a domain which accelerates the applications of AI Machines that can see. AI Machines can now perceive their surroundings just as humans can without any support. There is a Japanese Machine named «AI Guardsman» which can detect troubling behaviours and alert shop-owners to potential shoplifters. The companies behind «AI Guardsman» reported that the presence of this Machine has helped reduce shoplifting by 40%.

Another use is in the agricultural industry, which currently, is severely troubled by climate change, overpopulation and food security issues. One of the AI solutions working to resolve and lessen these effects is improving crop yield by reading the «health» of the leaves and adjusting fertiliser spray accordingly. This is being applied to reduce the amount of fertiliser used by nearly 40%.

AI Machines Write and Speak All Languages

The first chatbot was born in the mid-1960s, called ELIZA. It was created to imitate a psychotherapist who would paraphrase the patients' questions. The intent was to illustrate how human interactions could be superficial!

Only in the last five years have AI Machines been able to communicate. This development is mainly due to the Deep Learning algorithm that has also been used for image recognition programs. The best chatbot in the world, «Mitsuku,» underwent the Turing test and was shown to not have enough intelligence to understand the context of a question or conversation systematically. The Turing test has been used to evaluate the intelligence of chatbots since the 1950s and has indicated that AI Machines communicating with the same understanding as humans is not for the near future.

But even if an AI Machine is not yet able to communicate like a human, it can still perform some activities that will change the way we live. For instance, the language barrier between humans will soon disappear. AI Machines can translate Chinese and English live with the same quality as a top-notch translator. The translation is not the only way that AI Machines can be used for communication; they can write music partitions or even movie synopses, for example. They analyse past success patterns and write new creations to maximise the engagement of the consumer. There is no doubt that some productions, namely in marketing and communication, will soon be handled by Machines.

In 2018, we saw a massive increase in virtual agents that manage customer interactions by calls, chat or email. Even if AI Machines have not yet reached the level of humans in terms of contextualisation, they have more knowledge which, in many cases, compensates for their weaknesses. Most customer service agents have less information than the caller on the price, stock, process-ordering and of course, information on the caller themselves. With an AI Machine, being put on hold is no longer an option. The customer never has to wait for information or be transferred to a more experienced agent.

Virtual agents and assistants are now able to call or send emails to book flights or schedule meetings.

In 2018, Google demonstrated new features of their virtual assistant «Duplex» at their annual conference. Duplex is capable of making calls, in a male or female voice, performing only three tasks: checking for store hours, making restaurant reservations and booking hairdresser appointments.

Imagine a world without any language barriers.

AI Machines Can Digest Loads of Data for Better Predictions

In business, mathematical models and computer programs are commonly used to both predict and explain. In 1996, I founded my first company in predictive data modelling for three purposes: to optimise inventory management, define the right price for a plane ticket and to create financial products for investment banking. Then Big Data arrived in 2012. The flow of data from the internet and all types of sensors exploded. Data scientists were starting to be critical for organisations. Data science techniques could find solutions to complex business problems by combining mathematical algorithms with strong programming skills. According to Harvard Business Review, being a data scientist was the «sexiest job» in 2012.

Data scientists were also at the centre of the development of Artificial Intelligence. Even if AI Machines manage one-third of data scientists' jobs, by testing and adjusting the model, the data scientists will still tame the machines.

Of AI Machines with the capacity to predict, the approval of a patent called «anticipatory shipping», for Amazon in 2013, was a huge milestone. This is a system of delivering products to customers before they place an order. Having already transformed e-commerce with their «One-Click-Buying,» Amazon's next gamechanger involves Artificial Intelligence predicting your next click before you have done so. AI will use the patterns in your previous buying clicks to anticipate your next purchase. If this "Many-Click-Predicting" turns out to be wrong, the delivery will be offered anyway as a promotional gift to increase loyalty.

In the aircraft industry, the Internet of Things (IoT) creates new streams of data. The IoT allows parts of the plane to be connected with AI Machines. There are companies in this sector osing hundreds of billions of dollars every year to downtime issues. Instead of waiting for equipment to fail, AI Machines can predict and address problems of unrenewed or faulty equipment; this is called «predictive maintenance.» Predictive maintenance uses data from various sources, such as historical maintenance records, sensor data from Machines and weather data to determine when a plane will need to be serviced. Thanks to this AI function, airlines can increase the usage of every plane without compromising safety.

AI Machines are Starting to be On the Move

Movement is the biggest problem for AI Machines. Most predictions on the progress of Artificially Intelligent robots have not come to pass. For example, the most famous intelligent robot, named «ASIMO» and created by Honda in 2000, often seen at global conferences on technology or even playing soccer with the former President Obama, is dead. Even Google cancelled its project of a walking robot after the failure of the «Arm Farm», a manufacturing tool, which was intended to grab and hold objects.

Today, most robots are programmed to carry out a series of repetitive movements. Picking up an object and placing it elsewhere is a typical example, and it doesn't require any Artificial Intelligence.

However, 2018 saw the birth of a new perspective on Artificial Intelligence robots. The leader in this field is a company called Boston Dynamics, which introduced robots that could navigate through obstacles and react in real time to unexpected changes around them. New training data and algorithms support this kind of intelligence. In my mind, this is a new beginning for robotics.

Military defence is an obvious hotspot for the applications of mobile AI Machines. The use of AI Machines could drive all human forces off the battlefield. This would mean that defence budgets would shift greatly from human training and resources to the development of efficient combat robots. By 2019, the first step has been the deployment of ground AI robots that detect explosives, chemical, biological, radioactive and nuclear threats, as well as for reconnaissance missions.

We must stop presuming that AI Machines have to use human movement. There are different ranges of motions that are equally or even far superior to those nature has given us. AI Machines could be drones that fly like birds. An example is how AI algorithms now know, through their training, how birds use thermal updrafts to glide over long distances without flapping their wings.

One remarkable application of this new Intelligence into movement is the use of gliding drones to take close-up images in the protection of whales. The drones detect and survey whales like curious seagulls, flying so close they can collect mucus to identify their DNA, measure stress hormones and gain other insights into their health.

What Will the Collaboration Between Humans and AI Look like?

Beyond Fear, There is a Real Immediate Threat: Jobs

«Worrying about evil-killer AI today is like worrying about overpopulation on the planet Mars. Perhaps it'll be a problem someday, but we haven't even landed on the planet yet. This hype has been unnecessarily distracting everyone from the much bigger problem AI creates, which is job displacement.»

This is a quote by Andrew Ng, an adjunct professor of AI at Stanford who co-founded Google Brain and was a former VP and Chief Scientist at Baidu.

You can read a lot of reports and analyses on the impact of AI on the job market from Gartner, Forrester, McKinsey, PWC, Deloitte, World Economics Forum, and Stanford. Their forecasts before 2016 were pessimistic, but in 2019, we know that many of those forecasts were incorrect. The more recent predictions are either neutral or optimistic.

Most of these studies have some problems with relying on macroeconomic forecasts, but, more importantly, need punchline conclusions to attract the media. As for today, the consensus is the following: 20% of jobs will be destroyed. However, new jobs will compensate for that loss.

Just like with the digital wave, it is difficult to speculate on the jobs that will be created. 12 years ago, I was describing the job of a community manager to a group of executives. Even if we have started to identify the jobs that will be present in the future to monitor and maintain AI Machines, the new job descriptions and their quantity are still unclear.

So, I'm going to predict something about the company that you work for: in five to ten years, half of the activities that exist today will be performed by AI Machines. All repetitive activities, physical labour or intellectual, will be automated. We are talking about activities or tasks, not jobs. The number of current jobs that cease to exist will cap at 20%. Most human jobs have about 25% to 75% of their activities that can be handled by AI Machines. The impact on the workplace will be widespread and rapid. Most workers, from accountants to marketing directors to CEOs, will have to work with AI Machines. The workplace, business structures and workers' conditions will have to be reimagined.
What do you think would be the very worst case?

The Worst-Case Scenario: No Man's Business Land

The impact of AI on the workplace and its workers is going to change the concept of a company. The word «company» has an etymology arising from the archaic French military term «compagnie», meaning a body of soldiers. This French word was derived from Latin, as «your companion who eats bread with you.» Right now, the concept of a company is the uniting of human forces for a shared ambition, either private or public, profit or non-profit. This concept is evolving. Companies will soon be focusing on how to unify humans and machines for a common purpose.

Let's take the worst-case scenario of an AI Machine's implementation. Here is an example: a company in the financial industry called Lemonade Brothers. This bank processes a large amount of data, where the echelon of power is rigid with a culture of command and control. The short-term pressure on profit has incentivised Lemonade Brothers to use AI Machines to automate jobs. The speed of this deployment was swift and very successful. Short-term profit was achieved but came at the expense of employee engagement which is at its lowest ever. The organisation of Lemonade Brothers has become hyper-hierarchical with executives setting targets, and AI Machines overseeing the performance of all remaining employees with predictive analytics. Middle management has been reduced significantly because AI Machines are now controlling the lowest level of the business structure pyramid. The wage policy now has two poles: the executives earning options or shares of the profit increase, and the employees under the threat of losing their jobs to machines, and who encounter flat wages. The Lemonade Brothers scenario is imaginary; however, I have seen many companies heading in that direction.

The first example of this scenario was at a leading bank in Connecticut, USA at the end of 2016. The seats of the bank on one of the largest trading floors in the world had been replaced by a piece of paper on the floor saying the jobs had been displaced. The worst-case scenario I'm speaking of is not that of an organisation which fails in the implementation of AI. Rather, it is when an organisation creates half of its value from AI Machines while unmotivated people painfully drive the rest. This lack of motivation results in no control of AI Machines and no willingness to understand it. This is humans and machines in their worst light.

With the annihilation of the concept of what a company should be, the purpose of the employee has disappeared.
This is a «No Man's Business Land».

Neuron Organisation: To Value Human Potential

There is a tipping point where the concentration of AI Machines within a company will disconnect employees from the actual objective of the company itself. That just winded you. Essentially, when AI creates half of the company's value, all employees will naturally decrease their engagement. In the context of human capital no longer being the critical assets of a company, the employees' motivation and thus contributions will decline. Of course, the tipping point also depends on the size and culture of an organisation.

Business structures are designed to align the processes and people to achieve a common goal. What if AI Machines can achieve 50% of this goal? None of the current organisational models has an answer to this equation. Even though the digital wave shook up many traditional models of organisation, there is still a lot of rigidity due to unshifting cultures and sometimes inflexible IT systems. AI is transforming operations and in turn, will inevitably transform a range of markets and industries. A reorganisation of the workforce is imperative and will occur.

So, the question is: what is a successful model for an organisation where AI Machines create half of the value of a company?

Let me introduce you to what I will call «Neuron Organisation,» or «Neuron Org,» as the business structure that fosters the harmonious relationship between humans and AI Machines.

In this model, AI Machines have amplified the human capabilities needed in the workplace; therefore, humans are happy and open to working with Artificial Intelligence. It will be a mutually beneficial relationship feeding off the core strengths of both the humans and AI Machines. They will have a common interest in the success of the organisation and in fulfilling the objectives of the company.

Why a Neuron Organisation?

Artificial Intelligence recreates the neural network in the biological central nervous system. Neurons are the lowest common denominators between humans and AI. They both activate their intelligence by connecting neurons through electrical signals that vary in strength and speed, akin to the Neuron Org workplace structure. The intelligence of humans and AI Machines will be connected and stacked upon each other in the Neuron Org. I will explain how in the next chapter.

ORGANISATION DESIGNED FOR HUMANS

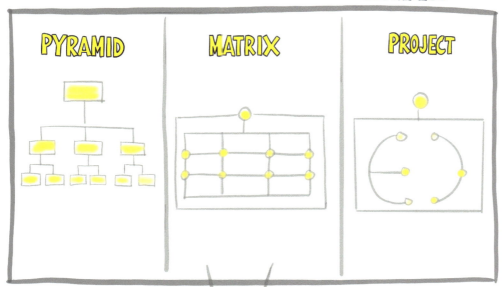

PYRAMID   MATRIX   PROJECT

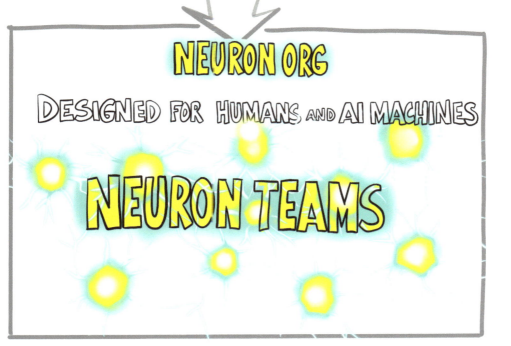

NEURON ORG

DESIGNED FOR HUMANS AND AI MACHINES

NEURON TEAMS

The Silhouette of Neuron Organisation

The conceit of Neuron Org is to rediscover the value of the collective effort, the «body of soldiers.» A small and agile team is generally successful. Let's assume a team of eight to 12 people is sustainable, called «Neuron Teams.» In these Teams, spirit and collaboration are flying well above current standards, enabling each member to take on a variety of roles. The hierarchy has been reduced to its minimum. The Neuron Team has AI Machines fully embedded and monitored by humans.

There will be numerous Neuron Teams within Neuron Org, each dedicated to a strategic focus within the company. To exemplify, there will be separate Neuron Teams committed to customers, supply chain, production, back offices and research and development.

Each member of these Teams has developed a capacity for interaction and collaboration with AI Machines. They know what they want, how they will get it, and then get what they want. AI Machines are treated as colleagues.

The disappearance of separate databases will set in motion the transformation of all data processes. The result of having minimal hierarchy is that companies will be able to focus on a critical area without getting lost in the vastness of the company structure or politics. For example, there is no need to have three separate departments in marketing, customer services and communication; they will all merge within the one customer Neuron Team. With new strategic objectives, a new Neuron Team will emerge and quickly connect with the rest of the organisation. After all, neurons that fire together wire together.

AI Machines will have easy-to-read interactive screens indicating what they're processing so that humans can be aware of what the Machines are doing. However, humans and AI Machines will communicate verbally, just like a human working with another human.

As in biology, neurons are either active or passive, which aligns with the two types of activity for the Team members. In active mode, people will collaborate with AI Machines to perform their work, activities and in general, the mission of the company. They will interpret and validate the input of the Machines, problem-solve, and develop new business scenarios.

The passive mode is the other course of action, where humans direct their effort to heighten their capabilities. People will be able to free themselves for some time to review the performance of the Machines, discover new technologies, or innovate. This is possible due to the efficiency of the AI Machines working 24/7. The passive mode will represent one-third of people's time at work.

On that account, workers will dedicate themselves to learning how to keep up with AI Machines which are also constantly evolving. They will strive to acquire the skills necessary to work as an individual and in a Team. There will be a dedicated Human Development Centre to help this goal flourish, demonstrating the company's investment in human capital.

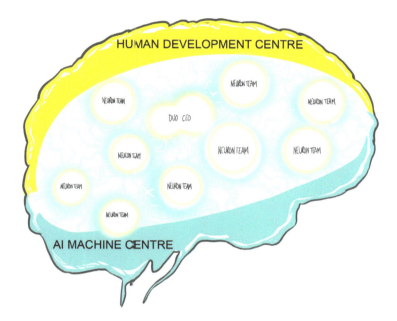

In parallel to the Human Development Centre for workers, there will be an AI Centre for training, controlling and repairing AI Machines. Its central purpose is to secure and enhance the relationship between Neuron Teams and AI Machines to create an efficient, holistic workplace. Teams within the AI Centre will guarantee the performance of AI Machines by expanding the boundaries of each algorithm. They will build the Machines and ensure their data security and reliability. The new jobs AI creates will be hosted in this crucial section of the company, like the cortex of a human brain.

Within Neuron Org, human beings through Neuron Teams are accountable for making decisions. A duo of CEOs will monitor operations and the business organisation, only intervening in the case of conflict or dysfunction. Why the duo? Firstly, half of the company will work 24/7 and this increase in data will force more decisions to be made. It won't be feasible to place such pressures on only one leader. Secondly, a duo will allow one CEO to focus on the efficiency of Neuron Org, and the other on the purpose of the company and application of their ethical rules.

The organisation structure of Neuron Teams and a duo of CEOs avoid there being a conventional layering of management, which in turn enables decision making at a speed that the customer or market demands. To have two CEOs means to be ready for this transformation.

Welcome to Humain Inc.

How Humain Inc. Has Realised Neuron Org

«Fortune favours well-prepared minds», said Louis Pasteur, a famous French biologist.

To avoid the worst-case scenario - AI Machines deteriorating the company processes and employee engagement - the entire organisation must change. Even if there is some congruity between the digital wave and the newborn Artificial Intelligence in terms of innovation and the speed of change, the transformation will be much more profound this time with AI Machines. Prepare for the double impact: on the organisation of processes and on workers' conditions. This change is so unique that it is bound to go down in history. Many are already dubbing it «The Fourth Industrial Revolution». A large proportion of employees will have to stop performing their tasks and give them up to AI Machines. Some will be required to change their occupation. However, all of them will have to be capable of working with AI Machines by developing new skills. This transition could be harmful like it was for Lemonade Brothers, but it can also be smooth like it was for Humain Inc..

Originally, people were scared of change. Humain Inc. used AI Machines to take over some tasks and perform to this new operating model. The conversation of Humain Inc. employees has shifted from being replaced by AI Machines to trying something entirely novel. Some people were being displaced and retrained to work with AI Machines; others were recruited to accelerate the collaboration between humans and Machines.

To manage the well-ordered propagation of AI Machines, Humain Inc. has realised the impact that AI will have on people and their work. The transition will occur at the same speed and depth at every level of the company, which is the challenge. Typically, companies transform from the top of their organisational structures to the bottom, or vice versa, and not as a whole. I will now describe the key dynamics of Humain Inc. in its journey.

Humain Inc. has one central team to set up AI Machines. In this team, AI experts are not only tasked with setting in place and managing the Machines, but they also spend half of their time preparing the rest of the company. They are also tasked with training and educating humans. This central team will have to build and manage data assets. Most of the time, the quality of data is worse than the organisation realises. In many cases, data is sparse, erroneous and incomplete. In my experience, I have observed that enhancing the quality of one's own company data and accessing the right external data is a necessity for building efficient AI Machines.

Overall, the central team progressively has disappeared and the organisation has formed more Neuron Teams, new multidisciplinary teams using AI Machines.

As more and more neurons have began developing in Humain Inc., the collective intelligence of the workforce has exploded. What could be a smarter and more efficient workplace than a whole brain operating at peak efficiency?

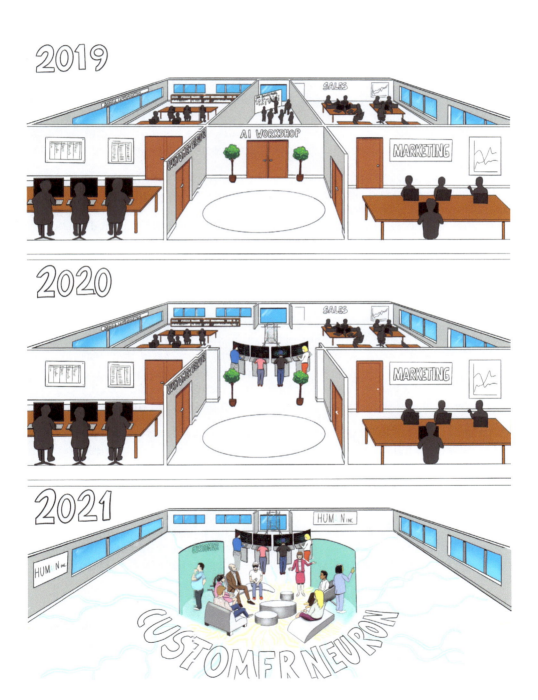

The Collaboration of Humans and AI For the Good of Society

In a world where AI Machines will create a significant part of a company's value, human employees must be engaged. This is vital for the health and sustainability of a business. In the last few years, some large companies have introduced purpose concepts to operate their businesses. The results have been positive in terms of employee commitment, the retention of high performers and market capitalisation.

I am convinced that in the presence of AI Machines, the organisation of businesses will aspire to do more 'good' for society. This involves shifting from purely financial targets to incorporating social and environmental goals. In recent years, Environmental, Social and Corporate Governance (ESG) criteria has gained traction in corporations setting sustainable and ethical goals in their agendas. Some companies are now searching for this «purpose formula».

What is Humain Inc.'s purpose formula?

The purpose formula is more than just creating thick documents on ESG criteria. Humain Inc. has created a declaration of the social impact of their business, outlining their mission and related objectives. These objectives will serve their stakeholders beyond just financial profit-seekers. The success of Humain Inc. is measured on qualitative criteria beyond financial indicators, including employee engagement, talent retention and the share of people who find meaning in their work.

Many organisations have already started down the path of purpose, yet with alternate motivations. A reason why many leaders introduced these measures was to reduce attrition and retain high performers, whereas others did so because it was part of the founder's vision. The purpose of a company's strategy is to be an attractive magnet for talent and to anticipate the impacts AI Machines will have on their organisation. Even some country leaders, such as Jacinda Arden, the Prime Minister of New Zealand, have decided to take this path of purpose. She stated at Davos in 2019 that New Zealand will no longer measure the progress of the country solely through GDP, but rather with «the wellbeing budget», which measures the impact on the wellbeing of the population, including health, pollution, social and environmental targets beyond just financial measures.

No business will perform solely based on the value created by AI. Businesses will only be able to promote their services or products with a healthy relationship between humans and Machines. For this collaboration to bear well, humans must align themselves with an authentic and higher purpose that coincides with the mission of the company, guiding them when making important decisions. That is the purpose formula, and with it, we now have an organisation with AI Machines and humans who are motivated and successful.

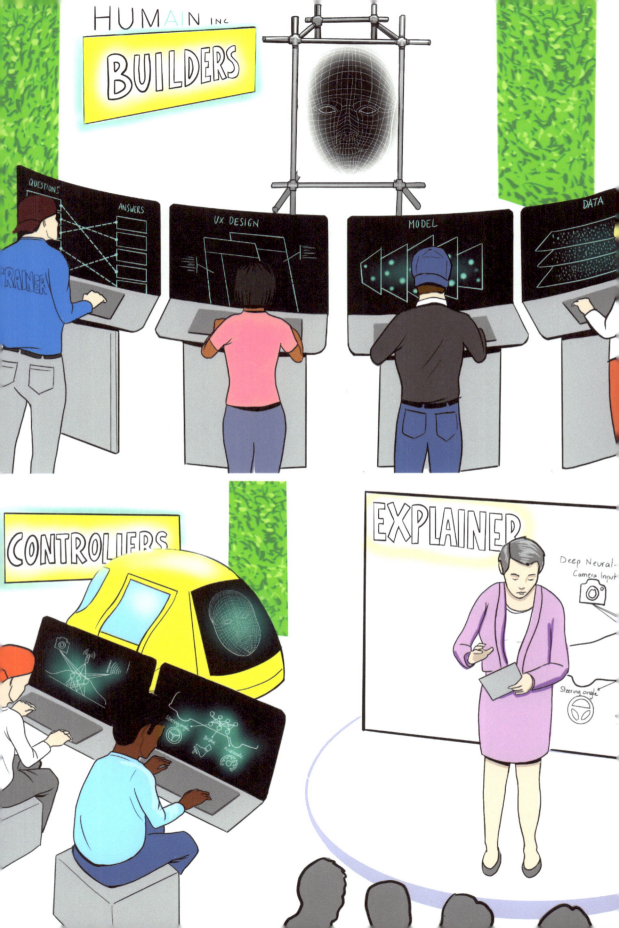

New Jobs will Augment Collective Intelligence

Artificial Intelligence will evolve quickly, like the brain of a healthy baby. The current models associated with supercomputing such as neural networks and Deep Learning will eventually reach the end of their purposeful lives. I believe that new models will appear but this time, with new computing powers like «quantum computing», a breakthrough towards using more data with less electricity. The speed of innovation surrounding tech is rapid, exponential, and is the reason why humans must upskill now. New skills should be adopted to properly manage AI Machines and also to enhance human performance in their presence.

What are the key capabilities of Humain Inc.?

There is a critical skill called defining «the problem statement», one that is often forgotten. Asking the AI Machine to fix a specific problem is not a simple task. When you present a fellow human being with a problem, you do not have to be 100% explicit. On the other hand, you must be with an AI Machine.

Data skills are not new but are critical for humans and will continue to evolve. All Humain Inc. workers understand the lifecycle of data. Data skills including statistics, programming and visualising are mandatory, as well as understanding the flow of data and what is creating it.

An example of a new job that masters both problem statements and data management is the «AI Trainer.» Being an AI Machine Trainer does not require any skills to do with actual teaching, it means being able to master data with a highly rigorous approach and to annotate large datasets.

Once the AI Machine has been built, it must be tightly managed. To control an AI Machine, human workers must be able to supervise it and understand how the Machine has created the outcome. This need is creating a new role: AI Machine Controller, one which requires a solid foundation in mathematics on top of communication skills. AI Machine Controllers will ensure that the Machine is fed with the correct data. They will adjust and refine the model if bias has distorted its results, or if the business objectives have changed.

For the time being, some AI algorithms are impossible to explain because the Machine evolves with the flow of data inserted into them. The AI Machine Controllers will have to justify themselves when they are unable to explain the outcomes of AI Machines. Last, but not least, the controller will have to warn the organisation if the code of ethics has been breached or tampered with.

AI MACHINE BUILDERS

TEAM PROFILE

Embrace an inclusive culture

KEY ACTIVITIES

| Translate business ambition into AI goals | Test Algorithm | Train Algorithm | Prepare database | Design interface between machines & humans |

SKILLS

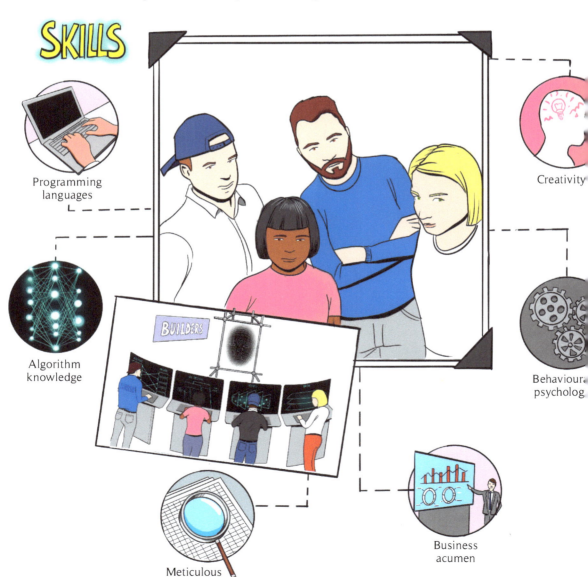

Programming languages

Creativity

Algorithm knowledge

Behavioural psychology

Meticulous

Business acumen

AI MACHINE CONTROLLERS

TEAM PROFILE
Make everything explicit

KEY ACTIVITIES

| Explain performance | Guarantee ethics compliance | Refine algorithm | Control data input & output |

SKILLS

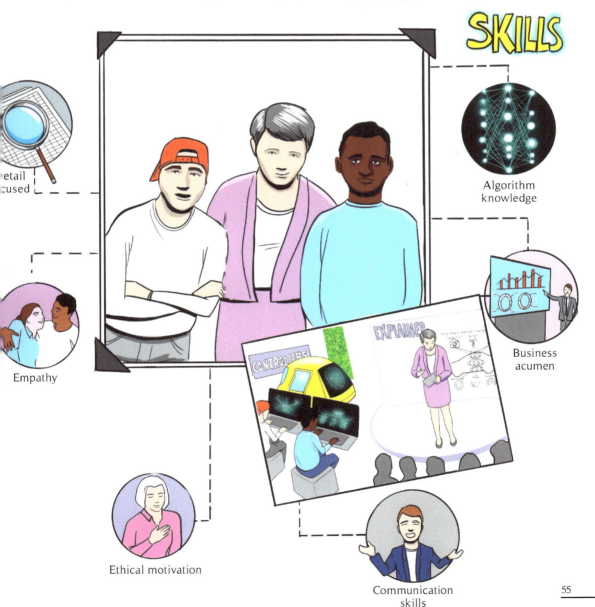

Detail focused

Algorithm knowledge

Empathy

Business acumen

Ethical motivation

Communication skills

55

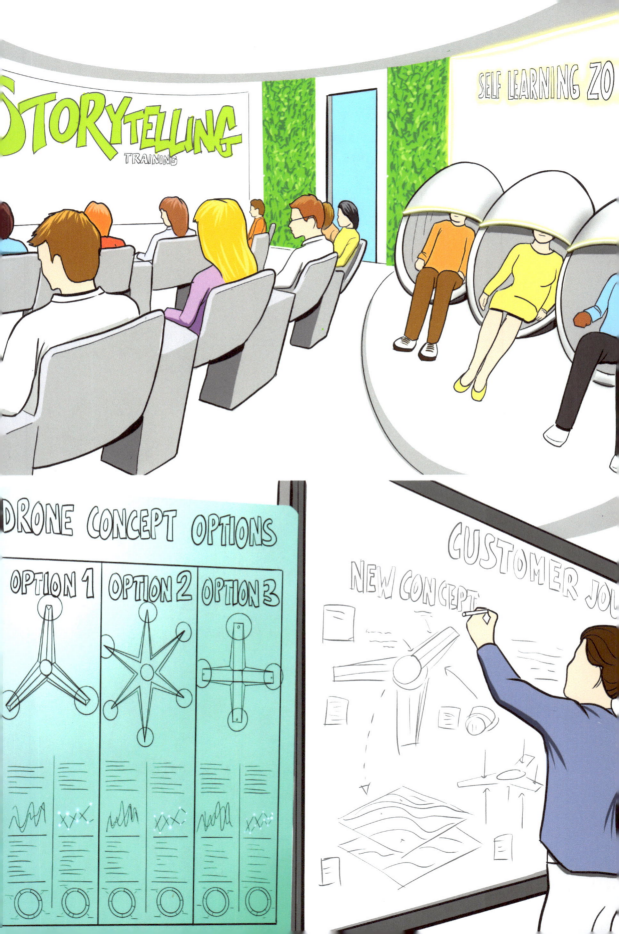

AI Machines Never Stop Learning; Humans Will Have to Follow

Humain Inc. knows that to stay competitive, it must continually learn.

Companies believe that to remain competitive they must learn and improve their organisation each and every day. The reality is far from that. Spending on workplace training has been declining for two decades and the gap between the knowledge of the current workers and state-of-the-art technologies is widening. Therefore, humans will have to be trained quickly to match what AI Machines are bringing to the table.

The shift in our times - of working with AI Machines - is an opportunity to reset our current behaviours and increase our desire and aptitude for learning. AI Machines love failures because they cannot learn without them. To learn continuously, they must make mistakes. On the other hand, many humans have been conditioned to fear failure, which triggers painful emotions such as shame or anger. In turn, humans tend to avoid learning procedures and quickly give up. If they make too many mistakes, they will hide those mistakes from the organisation. If humans are forced to fear failure, it is mostly irrational, and the conclusion is too often «bad fortune.» This limits humans' ability to learn. AI Machines learn from their failures, enhance their algorithms and find better solutions. They look forward to what we have been conditioned to avoid.

The presence of AI Machines in Humain Inc. has allowed humans to be more human, having been liberated from the physical, repetitive or transactional tasks which once plagued them. This only happened when they began to understand why they, as humans, were unique, with the traits of creativity, emotional intelligence, empathy, critical and systems thinking. The most crucial element when training humans to leverage the contribution of AI is creativity. Think of an automated world where algorithms are central; creativity will be essential. Creative thought is the engine of innovation, and whilst natural to children, can be taught to adults. Steve Jobs, the co-founder of Apple, once said: «Creativity is just connecting things.»

As the future will revolve around Artificial Intelligence, a critical application of creativity will be storytelling. To connect with people on an emotional level is one of the beautiful things that can never be taken away or displaced by any artificial force. Telling stories will be one way to balance the presence of AI Machines with a good dose of humanity.

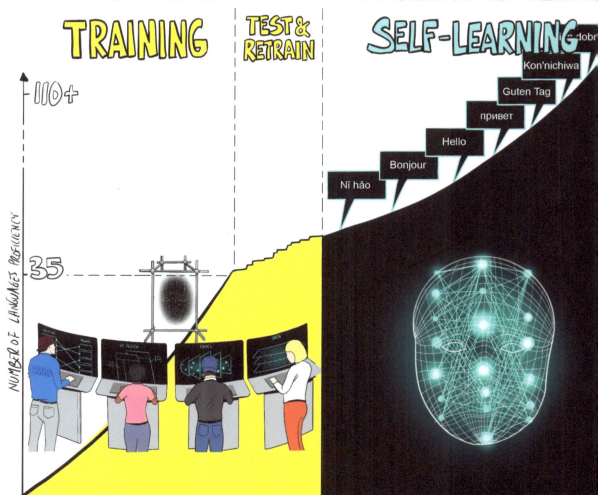

AI is the New Black Box

When one human doesn't understand another human, they are in the grey zone. Some of the most successful entrepreneurs in the world use the grey zone to their advantage. When a human doesn't understand the goings of some technology, the technology is a black box, closed shut.

For over 20 years, I have worked in consulting and technology businesses and I am continually amazed by how some organisations justify their inability to handle changes driven by technology. Most of the time, information systems don't create the value they were supposed to bring, and when it needs modification, the common response is: «We cannot modify it easily. It is a black box. The people who developed it are no longer available.»

Companies will never get the full value of their information systems if the coding and pool of data are not understood from the beginning. The black box syndrome is a reality and has been used too often to evade change in technologies. Such companies are bound to become obsolete.

The black box syndrome worsens in the presence of AI Machines because there is a mix of mathematical modelling and code development required to achieve business outcomes. Let's start with AI code development.

Most of the developments require a solid knowledge of libraries - code that has already been written to minimise confusion and effort, near to a copy and paste. The black box effect won't exist if small pieces of code are understood by the wider community, rather than just IT specialists.

The black colour of the box comes from the AI algorithm, Deep Learning. With this kind of algorithm, it is easy to know what data is entered and what the outcome is, but no one knows what happens in between. All the tech Giants recognise this weakness. Google acknowledges that they are still struggling to understand the Google translator algorithm. Initially, the translator was only trained for 35 languages and can now translate over 100 different languages without requiring any further training. Another example is when the CEO of Google, Sundar Pichai, once had to explain to Congress why a Google search of «idiot» resulted in images of Donald Trump.

At Humain Inc., AI Machines are equipped with algorithms that are easier to understand, hence a better prediction accuracy, while maintaining the utmost performance. Humain Inc. performs regular control checks (internal or third-party) to ensure utter transparency, thus control. This avoids potential issues to do with the Machines before they occur. and importantly maintains a sense of trust between Humain Inc. workers and its Machines.

Many humans have a tendency to accept the fact that people can be wrong, but always expect technology and AI Machines to be faultless. We mustn't forget AI Machines are a human creation.

A Unique AI Machine with Organic & Healthy Data

Deep Blue defeated Gary Kasparov in 1997. Six years earlier, IBM had created a dataset of 700,000 chess games played only by masters. Behind the success of every AI Machine, there is a hidden data breakthrough.

Today, 80% of the workload in setting up an AI Machine relies on the development of the database. It must be the right data for building, testing and running the Machine. The quality of the Machine is inextricable from the quality of the data; they can't be separated. The software or code will be easier and easier to get, although the real entry barrier is the ability to attain and manage the data.

The very first dataset is vital to train the AI Machines, provide the input and output, and to ensure that the AI Machine will start to build its model. It is at this stage that the profile of the AI Machine is created. For example, to build a chatbot, you must create a dataset with all possible questions and expected answers. It is with those thousands of questions and answers that you will shape the style and method in which the Machine will represent the brand. This is the training phase. The data could come from internal or external sources, internet usage, social media statistics, any form of online communication, services or connected devices. This mass of data is the commotion you read about in the media - Big Data and its big data. 90% of the world's existing data has been generated in the last two years.

Following this trend, many companies have implemented some Big Data projects, creating deep data lakes. A data lake is a system where all the company's data is stored in its natural format. AI Machines cannot swim, so throwing the AI Machine into the data lake and expecting it to create value, let alone survive, is not a good idea. The data needed to nurture your AI Machine must be cleaned, organised and stored methodically. It must be «healthy» data.

One of the illustrations of the impact of not building the right data set for AI Machines is facial recognition. In this particular case, facial recognition interprets emotion. This AI Machine could be used for recruitment, fraud detection or public safety. At the beginning of 2019, while facial recognition works perfectly to interpret emotion for white people, it is still struggling for Asian people and those with darker skins. The AI Machine is only as smart as the data used to train it. If there are many more white men than black women in the system, it will be less efficient at identifying black women.

With AI Machines, we are entering a new dimension of data volume and sensitivity with millions or even billions of records of past transactions, for instance, at a brokerage or medical records. The privacy and protection of data is now a significant concern for all companies, including Humain Inc. It would be a shame to see paddocks of blooming flowers damaged by a foreign virus because of poor cultivation. Data is the same; it is precious. takes hard work to put together and must be organic.

Make Ethics Serious

Humain Inc. faces two, core ethical challenges. Firstly, the workers may try to use AI Machines for malicious means. Secondly, the Machines may try to diverge from their peaceful purposes, requiring a new type of control. Both humans and AI Machines are being closely supervised within Humain Inc in this respect.

History has not portrayed favourably the organisations which prioritise short-term profits over morals. Companies in energy, tobacco and financial services have not all established a clear code of conduct in the last 15 years. We don't need AI to detect a clear pattern in this case. Our new situation must place ethics at the top of our agenda, rather than following the trends of moral apathy as shown in the Lemonade Brothers case.

Posting a list of values or «purpose» on the company website or the fridge is not enough. The code of conduct and ethical guidelines in the presence of AI Machines must be explicit and public, as they are in Humain Inc. In 2015, the ethical guidelines and rules in Google's AI teams were not explicitly defined, leading to Google Photos' algorithms labelling black humans as «gorillas». This could and should have been avoided. Today, we must define a new set of rules. Amazon has abandoned the use of AI Machines for recruitment because the dataset reflected a preference for hiring males. This was pointed out only by the team who built the AI Machine.

Rules can't only be applied to the humans building the Machines, they should extend also to those defining the objectives of the Machines. In 2018, an AI team at Stanford claimed they created an AI Machine that could distinguish gay and heterosexual people based on their facial features. The algorithm was supposed to detect the specific traits of narrow jaws and longer noses to elaborate a pattern. Their ethics code should have validated the intent of the human before asking the Machine such questions.

At Humain Inc., the Ethics Committee has ensured that all control processes are in place before AI Machines start becoming autonomous. In the AI Centre, the teams who build and test AI Machines are versed in anthropology and sociology, meaning that they have an understanding of humankind and the mechanics of our societies. Ethics and morality differ across countries and cultures, and that is the reason why Humain Inc. has published a specific code of ethics - to set new, serious expectations for the ethics of humans and AI Machines.

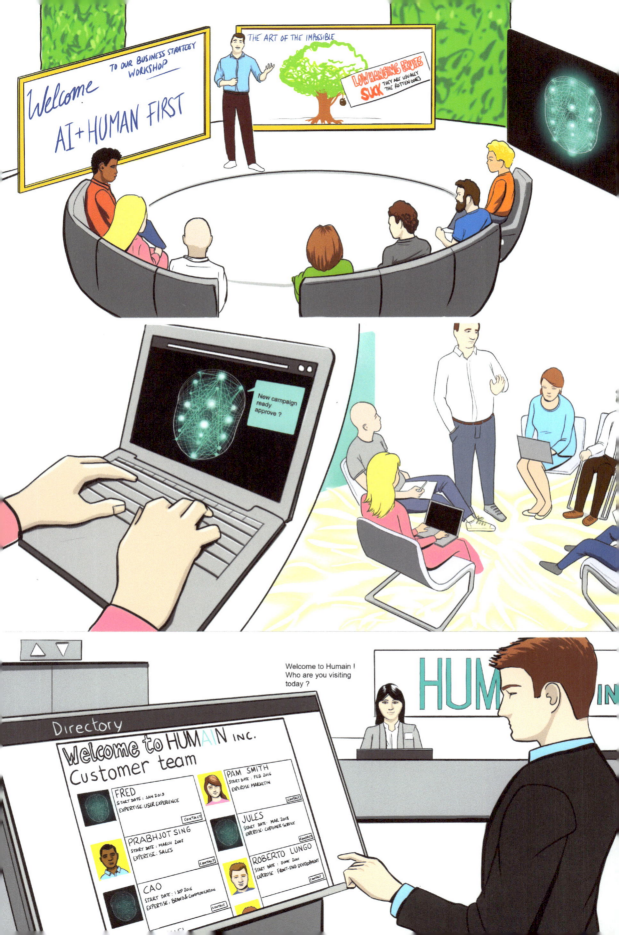

The Cogs of Human and AI Collaboration

At a large global company, I overheard the following question at the coffee machine: *"Is it true that machines will replace us?"*
Someone responded: *"Yes. I heard the experiment was successful."*

A lack of trust and transparency is not a great start to any relationship. Humans and AI Machines must avoid this problem.
The trust issue is arising also from the implementation of Artificial Intelligence.
Too often, I witnessed companies that had a «low-hanging fruit» mentality.
A typical example of this type of mindset would be for companies to build an AI Machine to carry out simple tasks that a human could easily perform. This strategy will inevitably damage the synergies between humans and Machines but also undermine the potential of AI machines.

Humain Inc. has brought AI Machines into its organisation, not as just an IT project, but as part of their recruitment process. They know that their first step is to define an ambitious goal. An AI machine with a simple algorithm and a well-picked dataset performs complex processes and tasks that the human workers can't. Humain Inc. has quickly realised that AI Machines actually encounter more difficulties performing an easy task than harder ones. That is, easy tasks in the light of human ability. AI Machines have surfaced problems that would not have emerged under human responsibility because the solution is not within their capabilities. Therefore, by defining ambitious goals at Humain Inc., the collaboration between humans and AI Machines is strengthened.

To collaborate with AI Machines means having interaction. That's why all interfaces between humans and AI Machines are critical at Humain Inc., in order to avoid any weak links. At Humain Inc., the juncture points between humans and AI Machines have been designed to grant the workers control over the datasets, adjusting algorithms and understanding the outcomes. One fundamental interface is at the moment when AI Machines take action and require authorisation from humans. The success of this event is critical for a trusting relationship. The workers of Humain Inc. can approve the action via verbal instruction, a click of their mouse or even just by nodding their head as you would to a colleague.

In the spirit of collaboration, the AI Machines of Humain Inc. are considered a valuable part of the organisation. They have names, are visible to the whole organisation for their role and the team they belong to. Their performance is reviewed in the same way as any Humain Inc. worker would be.

No AI Machine Can Predict the Future of Humans

AI Machines are here, their progress will carry on and nobody can predict how far it will go. Machines are already in your smartphone and are moving swiftly from the consumer's world into the workplace. However, fearing AI Machines and slamming on the brakes is not an appropriate reaction. We must be quick to adopt and adapt to these AI Machines. The advantages are clear and it would be short-sighted to fear these changes. The benefits will be numerous for both companies and individuals. Companies will be able to maximise profits together with achieving social and environmental goals, and humans will ideally have longer, healthier lifespans and enjoy a higher standard of living.

AI Machines will manage more and more activities. We will have to learn to level ourselves with Machines in terms of knowledge surrounding computer science, data analysis and statistical techniques. Of course, some jobs will be displaced but some will be created. The value creation will increase rapidly and during this transition, the workers should get their fair share. In past decades, the lack of income growth compared to the growth of company profits has created a wide polarisation of wages. With AI Machines there is a risk this may worsen, the risk being that the concept of the relationship between the company and the worker will be destroyed.

This transition may be painful and even more so if it is not well managed. The ambition is to enhance the workers' quality of life and enhance human creativity to eliminate all the «outs» in business: burnouts, bore-outs and brownouts.

Humain Inc. found the solution to the threat against working conditions by implementing Neuron Org, resulting in a fruitful collaboration between workers and Machines. At Humain Inc., the machine has been removed from the human to enable workers to amplify their goals and wellbeing.

It is difficult to have a consistent definition of Artificial Intelligence throughout the world. On top of that, it is hard for humans to place a definition on their own intelligence. So instead of defining or focusing on differences between the intelligence of humans and Machines, we must use Artificial Intelligence to amplify and extend our own; the intelligence of humans and Artificial Intelligence Machines are correlated. Believe me, a Machine told me.

Far out in the wild and unseasonable backwaters of the Milky Way is an overlooked star. Orbiting this at a distance of ninety-two million miles is a highly photographed planet on which ages of evolution have produced a schizophrenic apex predator which speaks and having spoken, self-designates itself as human. A byproduct of humanity in the year 2019 is its creation dubbed Artificial Intelligence. It involves a stack of natural resources intricately put together in circuits. And it stands as the coexisting tool, enemy and friend of humanity.

Artificial Intelligence is a creature of nature. It is the evolution of things which Darwin spoke of but which was impossible to predict. We have come far from when humans came crawling out of the green, amino acid slime. This is where we are now, and it is not a make-it-or-break-it-point. It is a new world of optimism and opportunity, the Big Tech Bang.

Oscar Dumas

Know More

Five books that I recommend after reading HUMAIN:

- *Weapons of Math Destruction* by Cathy O'Neil
  Societal impact of algorithms

- *Superintelligence* by Nick Bostrom
  A classic to read, especially if you like the paperclip story

- *The Singularity Is Near* by Ray Kurzweil
  A very optimistic view of evolution of Super Intelligent machines

- *The Second Machine Age* by Erik (MIT) Brynjolfsson, Andrew (MIT) McAfee
  Impact of Artificial Intelligence of jobs

- *Neural Networks for Babies* by Chris Ferrie & Sarah Kaiser
  For parents who want to prepare their children for the future of work

Two thought leaders that I like to follow:

- Andrew Yan-Tak Ng is a Chinese American computer scientist, global leader in AI, inventor, business executive, investor and Silicon Valley entrepreneur who has made major contributions to artificial intelligence, deep learning, robotics, and machine learning. Ng co-founded and led Google Brain and was a former Vice President and Chief Scientist at Baidu, building the company's Artificial Intelligence Group into a team of several thousand people. He is an adjunct professor at Stanford University (formerly associate professor and Director of its AI Lab).

- Piero Scaruffi is an Italian American freelance software consultant and university lecturer who maintains a music website on which his reviews are published. Scaruffi also reviews many films. He has created his own publishing society called Omnipublishing that exclusively releases his books about music, cognitive science and artificial intelligence.

In humainthebook.com you will have access to some regular new insights and an updated gallery of drawings.

Acknowlegements

It takes a village to write a book for first time and so I have a lot of people to thank.

I will start with Oscar Dumas. I have had the privilege of working with Oscar to ensure that this book is accessible to everybody and anybody. His contribution was far beyond this though, as he brought his very personal style and humour to impress readers and produce an outstanding version of HUMAIN's vision.

Cleo Cardot is currently a student who shines brightly at the University of Sydney. She helped me to reduce the jargon and keep in mind that readers want simple explanations, not long textbook answers.

I would like to thank Prani, Ricky and Sau-Yeng for their proofreading and patient approach to working with francophone writing in English.

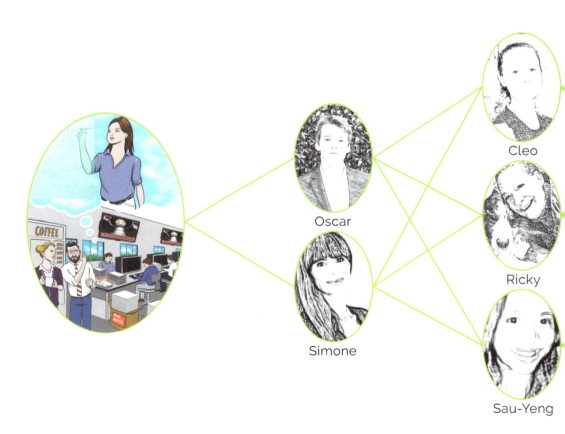

Oscar

Simone

Cleo

Ricky

Sau-Yeng

I was very lucky to meet Simone Planté at Bronte Beach that day. She has brought me her extensive Tech experience and coached me in many ways.

Audrey, my designer, has demonstrated once again her creativity and character with the design of this book, as she worked from the beautiful city of Aix-en-Provence.

Thanks, Cyril and Vincent for sharing your insights of the buoyant AI consulting market.

I cannot end the acknowledgements without giving some credit to my two boys, Gaston and Edgar, who continuously challenged and presented me with new ideas. This book is special because of them, even though they're only 12 and nine years old. Moreover, of course - I must and I will - thank their mother and my wife, Julie, for looking out for the boys and me, supervising and guiding me like a God from up above.

Thank you, all for being part of my Neuron Team.

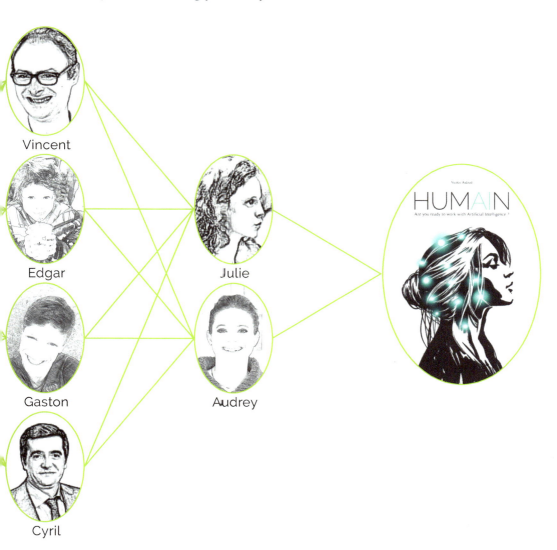

References

Bostrom, N. (2016). Superintelligence. Oxford University Press.

Bughin, J., Seong, J., Manyika, J., Chui, M., & Joshi, R. (2018). Notes from the AI frontier: Modeling the impact of AI on the world economy. Retrieved from https://www.mckinsey.com/featured-insights/artificial-intelligence/notes-from-the-ai-frontier-modeling-the-impact-of-ai-on-the-world-economy

Clifford, C. (2018). Bill Gates: 'A.I. can be our friend'. Retrieved from https://www.cnbc.com/2018/02/16/bill-gates-artificial-intelligence-is-good-for-society.html

Data Scientist: The Sexiest Job of the 21st Century. (2012). Retrieved from https://hbr.org/2012/10/data-scientist-the-sexiest-job-of-the-21st-century

Harden, J. (2019). The Wellbeing Of My Nation. Speech, Davos.

Hawking, S. (2014). Stephen Hawking warns artificial intelligence could end mankind [In person].

Jobs, S. (2019). Making Connections [Radio].

Kurzweil, R. (2005). The Singularity Is Near: When Humans Transcend Biology. Viking.

Ng, A. (2015). Nvidia's GPU Technology Conference [Radio]. San Jose, California.

Pasteur, L. (1854). Lecture, University of Lille.

US House Judiciary Committee VS Google, Sundar Pichai (US Congress 2018).

Text : Nicolas Aidoud
Design : Audrey Granier // a-graphic-design.com

www.ingramcontent.com/pod-product-compliance
Lightning Source LLC
Chambersburg PA
CBHW041428050326
40689CB00003B/697